Pie in the Sky

W9-CTT-173

Pie in the Sky
Lois Ehlert

SCHOLASTIC INC.

New York Toronto London Auckland Sydney
Mexico City New Delhi Hong Kong Buenos Aires

This tree
was here when
we moved in.

Dad says it's a pie tree.

I see
a blue jay feather
with black stripes
and a white tip,
and a green caterpillar
with a yellow band
and an orange false eye.
But no pie.

I've never seen pies growing on trees. Wouldn't that be something?

I see green grass, red ladybugs, red brown bark, and a blue green dragonfly. But no pie.

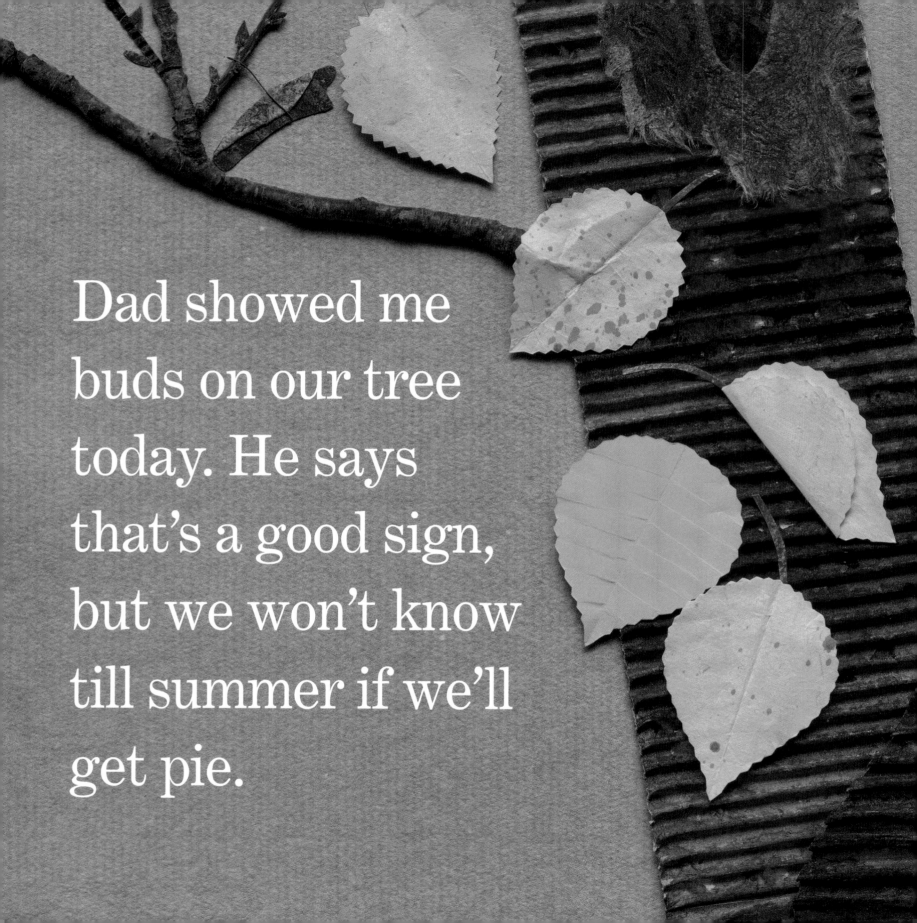

Dad showed me buds on our tree today. He says that's a good sign, but we won't know till summer if we'll get pie.

I see yellow leaves
with green spots,
brown buds,
a brown chrysalis,
and a gray snow sky.
But no pie.

Winter's finally over. Sweet spring is here at last. Buds we saw last fall are bursting into bloom.

I see
green leaves,
white blossoms,
yellow pollen dust,
blue eggs
in a brown nest,
yellow honeybees,
and black stripes
on a yellow
butterfly.
But no pie.

But now a damp wind
is blowing, and all
the flower petals
are falling down
like rain.

I see
white petals,
dark gray tails,
brown branches,
and a gray rain sky.
But no pie.

You know what? I think something's finally growing on that tree of ours.

I see orange and lime green balls, yellow moon and stars, a pale green moth, and a dark blue sky. But no pie.

The birds sure
sound excited.
I wonder what's
going on.

I see
a robin's rusty red breast
and white-speckled throat,
a gray catbird with a
black crown and tail,
and purple-violet clouds
in a pink-and-orange sky.
But no pie.

Uh-oh.

Now
I see.

I see
brown cherry pits,
red wing tips
on cedar waxwings,
and white rings
around robins'
black eyes.
But no pies.

It's a cherry feast!

I see
orange-breasted
orioles,
black spots and tips
on butterfly wings,
red ripe cherries,
and a bright blue sky.
But no pie.

But, hey, raccoon,
save some
for us!

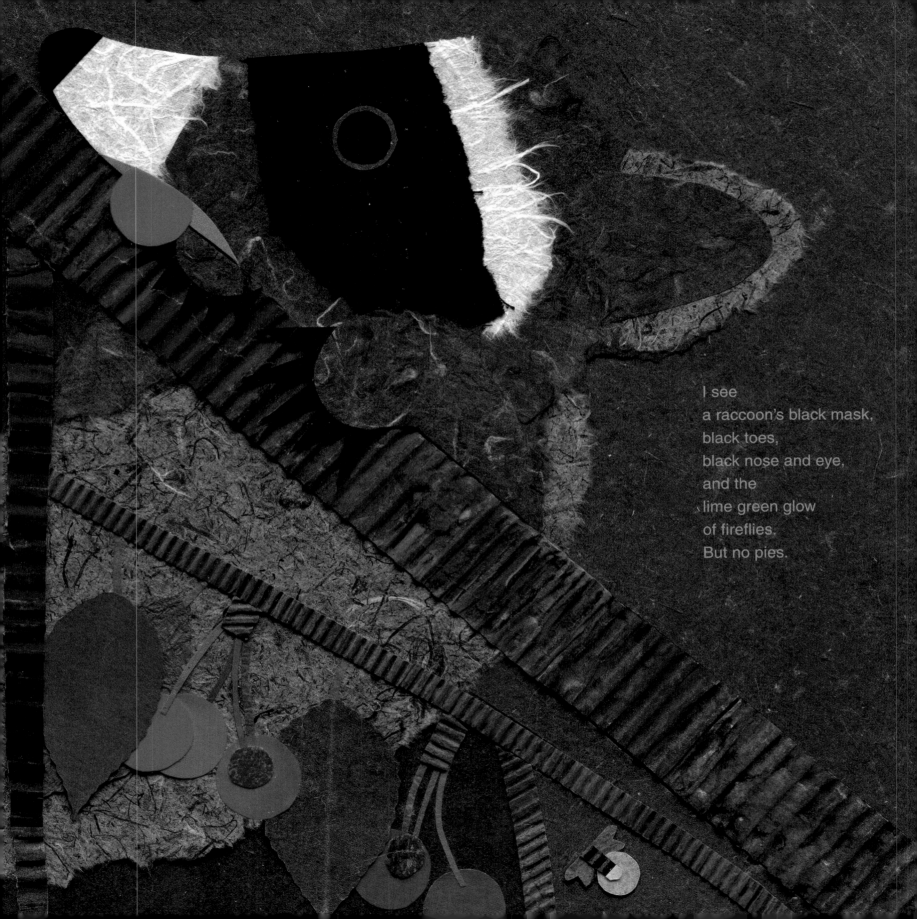

I see
a raccoon's black mask,
black toes,
black nose and eye,
and the
lime green glow
of fireflies.
But no pies.

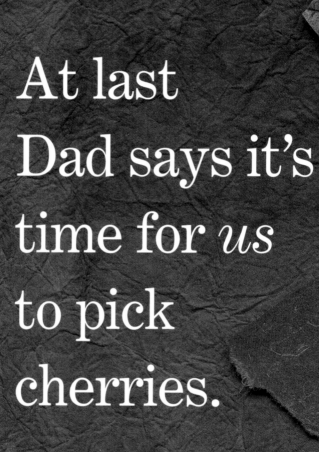

At last
Dad says it's
time for *us*
to pick
cherries.

I see
gray wings,
a black-and-orange tail,
a yellow beak,
a silver gray pail,
and a blue fly.
Still no pie.

We're
going
to make
a pie!

First we wash
the cherries.

4 cups
sour
red
cherries

We squeeze out
all the
pits

and
save
the
juice.

Then we put the cherries in a bowl.

½ cup juice

We add the juice, flour, sugar, and cinnamon, and stir it with a spoon.

5 tbsp. flour

1/3 cups sugar

1/2 tsp. cinnamon

Next we mix the piecrust dough.

We roll out two crusts
and press one
in the pan.

Then we pour the filling in.

9-inch pan

We add
the top crust,
put the pie
in the oven,

and
wait
for it
to bake.

Press around crust edge with a fork to seal.

Cut design into crust so steam can escape while baking.

Preheat oven to 450°. Bake 10 minutes.

Reduce heat to 350°. Bake 35 to 45 minutes, until brown.

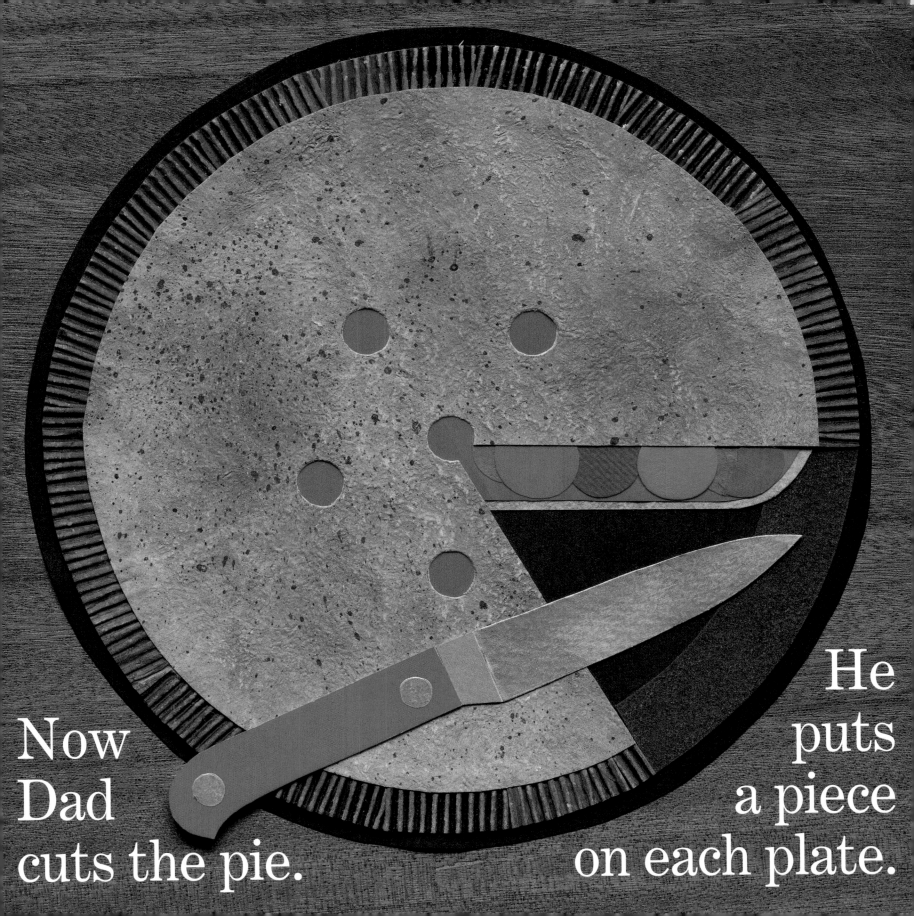

Now
Dad
cuts the pie.

He
puts
a piece
on each plate.

Wow!
That was
the best pie
I've ever
eaten.

I wonder if the
birds would like it?

No part of this publication may be reproduced, stored in a retrieval system,
or transmitted in any form or by any means, electronic, mechanical, photocopying, recording,
or otherwise, without written permission of the publisher.
For information regarding permission, write to Harcourt, Inc.,
6277 Sea Harbor Drive, Orlando, FL 32887-6777.

ISBN   0-439-70278-X

Copyright © 2004 by Lois Ehlert. All rights reserved.
Published by Scholastic Inc., 557 Broadway, New York, NY 10012,
by arrangement with Harcourt, Inc. SCHOLASTIC and associated logos
are trademarks and/or registered trademarks of Scholastic Inc.

12 11 10 9 8 7 6 5 4 3 2 1   5 6 7 8 9 10/0

Printed in the U.S.A   08

First Scholastic paperback printing, October 2005

With special thanks to all the cherry orchards of Door County, Wisconsin; Brightonwoods
Orchard, Burlington, Wisconsin; University of Wisconsin Cooperative Extension Offices,
Milwaukee and Sturgeon Bay, Wisconsin; Schlitz Audubon Nature Center, Milwaukee,
Wisconsin; Elizabeth Huntoon; Tom Rost; and Richard Ehlert (who made the cherry
wood heart). And to the cherry trees of yesterday that remain in full flower.

The collage illustrations for this book were made with acrylic and watercolor paints;
colored pencils; oil pastels; crayons; corrugated cardboard; handmade papers from
Japan, Italy, France, Mexico, and the United States; origami papers; Pantone coated
papers; vellum; wood veneers; sheet metal; wires; balsa wood; wax paper; and cherry
tree branches. These materials were glued, sewn, or wired to three-ply Strathmore board.

Designed by Lois Ehlert and Ivan Holmes